Lots of Laughing!

Learning lots of things

Happy thoughts at bedtime

Meet my baby brother Rafferty

Lovely Food!

Having Fun!

Let's be Friends

Special thanks to our children - William, Niamh and George. Their enthusiasm and interaction with Charlie and Rafferty made bedtime fun and have led to the writing of this book. And especially to my wife, Lyn, for encouraging me to write the book, for ideas, and for her patience and love.

Charlie & Rafferty

Publisher: Independent Publishing Network Ltd

ISBN 978-1-78972-855-2

'Charlie and Rafferty' is created by David Ellerton

Visit Charlie and Rafferty at www.charlieandrafferty.com

Say Hello to Charlie and Rafferty

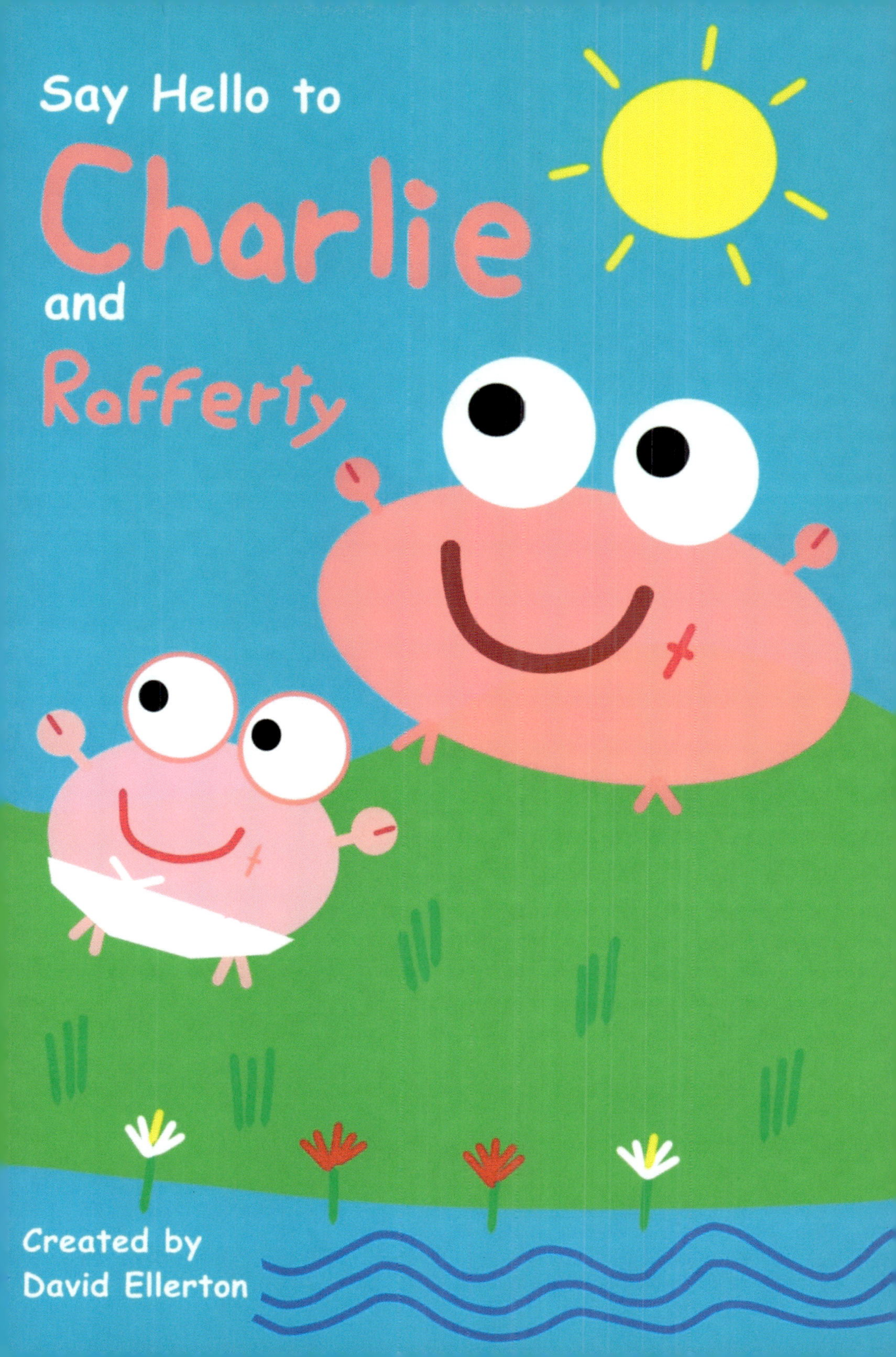

Created by
David Ellerton

For Will, Niamh
and George

For the Grown-Ups

Charlie and Rafferty are imaginary friendly crabs. Grown-Ups use their hand to talk as Charlie or Rafferty. Charlie and his new friend (your child) have fun conversations. Charlie is very inquisitive and asks lots of questions. He can also taste food. If he likes it, he'll say how nice it is. If he doesn't, that means a tickle!

The book guides you through the conversation. Change some of the questions as the conversation flows.

The book is written with Charlie asking questions. Harry is included in the book as an example. Swap your childs name wherever Harry is shown. The book is a guide - you can use the questions but your child will give different and unexpected answers.
Have fun!

Charlie - "Hello, I'm Charlie the Crab. What's your name?"

Harry - "Hello, my name is Harry."

Charlie - "Hello Harry, I've come to visit, just to say hello, because I live near-by."

Harry - "Oh, where do you live?"

Charlie - "I live near a stream not far away. You know, I've got lots of friends. I wanted to meet you so we can talk and learn about things."

Harry - "OK, what would you like to know about?"

Charlie - "What have you been doing today?"

Harry - "I've been to school."

Charlie - "What is school?"

Harry - "It's where you learn things."

Charlie - "What did you learn?"

Harry - "Reading, playing and drawing."

Charlie & Rafferty

I want to learn
about lots and
lots of things !

Charlie - "I've heard about numbers, but I'm not sure what they are?"

Harry - "Yes, numbers are on a clock."

Charlie - "What are numbers and what is a clock?"

Harry - "They help with being on time when you go somewhere so you're not late."

Charlie - "Oh I see, that's good, my mum tells me off when I'm late after playing with my friends."

Tick Tock Tick Tock

1

3

2

4

5

6

7

Numbers!

Charlie - "What else did you learn today?"

Harry - "I learned about the moon and the stars!"

Charlie - "WOW, what are they?"

Harry - "Well the moon is the big white round thing in the sky when you look up at night. It's bright and beautiful."

Charlie & Rafferty

Charlie - "That's a big word. I know what the moon is now though. I see it all the time when I'm going to sleep. What are stars?"

Harry - "You don't know what stars are silly! They are all the little white dots in the sky - friends of the moon!"

"They are small but shiny like the sun in the day time. They are a long way away my teacher said."

My friends

Charlie - "I wish I went to school as you learn lots. My mum and dad and friends all teach each other, about the stream and being outside, and having fun."

Charlie - "We'll have to talk lots more so we can learn lots more!"

Charlie - "I'm hungry. What did you have to eat today?"

Note for Grown-Ups

Charlie can taste food. If he doesn't like it, he'll tickle you. If he likes it he won't tickle and will try the next lot of food.

When Charlie is eating, he tickles gently. For example, if your child chooses number 1, Charlie will pretend to eat under your childs arm pit, and make a noise while he is eating. If he doesn't like the food, he will tickle more vigorously. Use the numbers below - these indicate where to tickle.

1 - is under arm, 2 - is tummy,
3 - is neck, 4 - is knee,
5 - is everything!

Harry - "I had lots of things."

Charlie - "Do you know I can taste
your food, but I'm not sure
if I will like it. Let's try."

Charlie - "Can I try some
food please."

Harry - "Yes of course you can."

Charlie - "Let's try number 1."
(munches under arm)
"What food is that?"

Charlie & Rafferty

1 3 5

2 4

Knee

Neck Tummy

Arm

Everything!

Urgghh! Yummy!

Tickle! Tickle! Tickle!

Harry - "It's a ham sandwich."

Charlie - "Urggghh, I don't like that."
(Tickle, tickle, tickle - under arm)

(Harry laughs a little)

Charlie - "Can I try some more food
please, let's try number 2."
(munches on tummy)
"What's that?"

Harry - "It's chicken."

Charlie - "Ummhh - I like chicken."
(Munches gently on tummy)

Charlie & Rafferty

No 1 - under arm

Urgghh!

Tickle! Tickle! Tickle!

No 2 - tummy

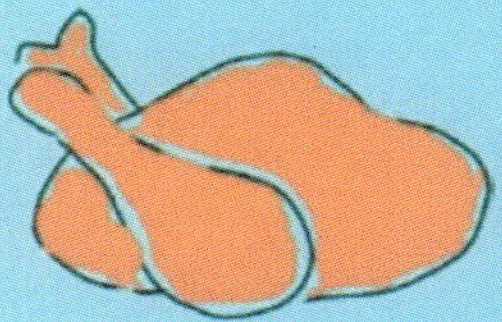

Yummy!

Umhh - I like that!

Charlie - "Can I have a drink

please - No 3?"

(Munches on neck)

Charlie - "What's that?"

Harry - "It's fizzy drink."

Charlie - "Urgggh - I don't
like fizzy drink."

(tickle, tickle, tickle - on neck)

(Harry laughs more)

Charlie - "Can I have another

drink please?"

Harry - "Yes, here's some water."

(Charlie still munches on neck)

Charlie - "Ummmhh - I like water."

Charlie & Rafferty

No 3 - neck

 Urgghh!

Tickle! Tickle! Tickle!

Try again

 Yummy!

Umhh - I like that!

Charlie - "I'm still hungry, can I have some more food please?"
(Munch on No. 4 - knee)

Charlie - "What's that?"

Harry - "It's a banana."

Charlie - "Urgggh - I don't like bananas!"

(tickle, tickle, tickle)

(Harry laughs a lot)

Charlie & Rafferty

No 4 - knee

I'm still hungry!

 Urgghh!

Tickle! Tickle! Tickle!

Charlie - "Right, I'm really hungry and thirsty. Can I try everything now please?"

Harry - "Yes, OK!"

Charlie - "Hoorah!!!"

(No 1, 2, 3, 4 and 5 - tickle, tickle)

Charlie - "Yum, yum, yummmyyy !!"

(Harry laughs a lot!!)

Charlie & Rafferty

1 2 3 4 5

Knee

Neck

Tummy

Arm

Everything!

Urgghh!

Yummy!

Tickle! Tickle! Tickle!

Charlie - "Thank you Harry, for teaching me things, and for letting me have some food and drink."

Charlie - "Can I come and see you again, and can I bring my little brother next time? He's a bit silly and very funny!"

Harry - "Yes, what's his name?"

Charlie - "His name is Rafferty, and he wears a nappy!"

Harry - "A nappy - is he a baby?"

Charlie - "I'm 5 years old. Rafferty is only 2 and he wears a big pull up nappy."

Charlie - "Rafferty also asks lots of questions, and he likes food even more than me!"

Charlie - "I'll bring Rafferty to see you next time."

Charlie - "Well, I've had a great time but I've got to go to bed now, so I'll see you next time."

Charlie - "Night, night, Harry, see you tomorrow and thank you for being my friend."

Harry - "Night, Night, Bye Charlie."

Charlie & Rafferty

The End

Lots of Laughing!

Learning lots of things

Happy thoughts at bedtime

Meet my baby brother Rafferty

Lovely Food!

Having Fun!

Let's be Friends

Printed in Great Britain
by Amazon

38312397R00020